Hi.
I'm Oliver

Told by Oliver (All Over My Heart) Wolfe
(Typed by my dad, Steven F. Wolfe, M.D.)

Huzon Fyrst Press
Mooresville, NC

Copyright© 2017 by Steven F. Wolfe, MD, Dermatologist
Cover Design: Carl Graves (Extended Imagery)

All rights reserved. Written permission must be secured from the publisher to use or reproduce any part of this book.

Author's Note

This book is a work of creative nonfiction. Any typos or grammatical errors are the fault of my dad, not me, OLIVER. I've only been to Puppy 1 and Puppy 2 class and have not yet learned typing or proper English. My dad says that even if there are typos or grammatical errors that the world isn't perfect. But he also says that it's a *lot* closer to perfect because of cute, smart, and adorable dogs like me.

ISBN-13: 978-0-9970483-2-2

Produced (by one of the cutest dogs) in the United States of America

Huzon Fyrst Press
Mooresville, NC

Introduction

My story is short (like me) and sweet (like me). I may only be two years old and weigh 9 pounds, but I'm smart, cute, and literary so I dictated my life story and my dad (Hi DAD!) agreed to type it for me since I haven't taken typing class yet. If you are reading this book, in all likelihood you either have a dog or love dogs (probably both), and everyone who has a dog or loves dogs knows that they really are man's best friend. So I hope that my book puts a smile on your face. Dad says if you buy a few copies he'll have more money to buy me new tennis balls, elk antlers, and toys, and send me to Puppy 3 school which includes typing class, so please share this book with everyone you know!

If you want to contact me check me out on Facebook:
@oliverallovermyheart
https://www.facebook.com/oliverallovermyheart/

I'm also online at
www.oliverallovermyheart.com

This book is dedicated to animals everywhere. Small and big, living in the wild or with a great family like mine, spoiled (like me), or having to fend for themselves. It is also dedicated to the people who care for and love them, like my parents. Mostly, it is to commemorate the idea of unconditional love given by pets like me to their owners. The idea that even if I am occasionally shunned because I did something I wasn't supposed to do (I REALLY am sorry about those two accidents I had in your bed Mom and Dad) I will ALWAYS come running back with my tongue hanging out and lick you in the face. Likewise, even if I haven't done anything wrong and you just need time alone (sadly meaning away from me) I will also come running back with my tongue hanging out and lick you in the face. Because in the end, all I really want is to give love and to receive it. Lastly, this book is dedicated to wonderful veterinarians (especially Dr. John, aka John Schaaf) and their assistants (Chris Jumper) and the great places that take care of astoundingly cute and wonderful pets like me (North Mecklenburg Animal Hospital). The compassion and love they have for pets, both while happy and healthy, as well as while they are declining, is extraordinary.

Oliver,
with WUF

Part I

Hi. I'm Oliver

Hi. I'm Oliver

THE BEGINNING

Hi. I'm Oliver. I'm the cutest, smartest, fastest Papillon, at least that's what my parents say. When they first met me, I was only 2 pounds 9 ounces and two months old. I didn't fuss ANY. Even when I had to leave my birth parents and go with my new (human) parents I didn't fuss.

I was born in Raleigh, North Carolina to parents who were champion agility dogs. So you see, even from the beginning, I came from champion stock, royalty if you will. Everyone knows that Papillons, the French word for butterfly, is a breed that royalty loved.

When my human parents picked me up, I smiled at them and licked them. When mom (Hi MOM!) picked me up and put me in her lap for the two hour ride home, I stayed in her lap. I napped, almost the whole way home. I might have been tiny and young, but I was a BIG BOY. I didn't cry. I didn't bark. I just nuzzled up against my mom's arm and let her other arm stay on top of me, protecting me. Dad (Hi Dad!) was so happy to have me he had some tears in his eyes. Tears of love.

As soon as I got to my new home I immediately peed. I had found the first of my new spots. All my mom or dad had to do was bring me there and I made a wee wee immediately. After I relieved myself, mom and dad brought me inside to their favorite room—the kitchen. And guess what? I had my own little house within the house—a brand new pint sized crate with a soft blankie. Since the door was open to it, I went right in—no invitation needed. And then you know what I did? Guess what? I laid down and stuck my head out on the metal grate at the front of the crate.

All Over My Heart

The door remained open and my head gently stuck partially out, supported by that metal grate and I did what any puppy would do. I went to sleep.

I'm going to take a nap. Night-night!

A couple of hours later I came out and my mom and dad played with me. I like to play. I love pull toys like ropes and squeaky toys, and stuffed animals and balls, and bones and socks (though nobody seems to leave these around for me as much as I would like). They seem to be Johnny on the spot if a *sock* falls on the floor…..maybe because I have special built in radar for socks on the floor?

TALKING TO THE LEASH

Right from the beginning my mom and dad placed a leash with a bell near the back door of the house and they liked to play with and talk to that leash with the bell. In fact, they would ding the bell and say: "do you have to potty?" I never knew why someone would talk to a leash and a bell— that leash and bell couldn't talk back or hear anything! Why even a young puppy knows that. Then they would turn to me and say, "Ollie, do you have to potty?"

They also had a game when I *got* to the door. They would hold my paw and ding the bell with my paw. It didn't take me long to figure out this game. Soon, I would ding the bell by myself. I was REAL smart. Now sometimes when I played ding the bell my parents would come in and be real happy. But the older I got, sometimes when I played this game they weren't so happy. They thought that the game ding the bell meant I had to go potty. Well, sometimes, I did and sometimes that's the way I played the game. But other times, the game was ding the bell so I could go out and play. These are the times they would come in and not be as happy. Oh well, sometimes I played the game THEIR way and sometimes I played it MY way. Sometimes I followed the rules………..sometimes I made them.

NASCAR

Since we lived in North Carolina, particularly near Race City (Mooresville), *and*, since my birth parents were champion agility dogs, it was only natural that I played NASCAR from the beginning. This is where I would run around the backyard and do figure eights and laps and quick turns. Sometimes I would just do it on my own, but it was ALWAYS more fun when dad would chase me. He was surprisingly fast and agile, particularly for a human, but I could still always run faster than he could. We both liked this game a lot. After a minute or two, I would just flop on my belly and stare at dad. We both liked this a lot. I would just lie on my belly and watch my daddy. I recovered lying on my belly. He would recover standing up. Then we would go inside and I would drink some water and usually walk into my crate and go to sleep with my head usually hanging out the front and resting on the grate.

Whenever it rained we played NASCAR *inside* instead of outside. The best was when dad would leave the two gates open to the kitchen. First we would start in the living room. I'd usually do a few laps around the coffee table, then I would beeline for the dining room, lap around the dining room table, and come back to the living room and the coffee table. Dad would chase me and clap and we were a hootin and a hollerin in no time. Occasionally, when dad chased me, I'd detour past the laundry room into the kitchen out of his site, lap the kitchen, and come back to the living room. Then dad would hide near the front door behind the partial wall from the dining room and I'd race up the other side of the wall and he would step out towards me and we'd do it all over again. And again. And again…until dad got tired because seemingly I could do this for a LONG TIME.

MY EARLY DAYS

My early days as a puppy I loved being with mom and dad. Sometimes dad would pick me up and hold me in his lap. In short order I would fall asleep. I liked to wrap my front paws partially around dad's forearm and rest my head on the crook of his arm in front of his elbow. It was very peaceful. Dad didn't know it, but I sometimes peeked at him when he wasn't watching and I could see a calm smile on his face. Our faces were both calm and both smiling. I thought you might want to see a picture of me as a puppy sleeping on dad's arm so it's on the next page.

Mom also liked to hold me on her lap. I would sleep often for an hour or two and not fuss *any*. Just like when I was on dad's lap, I sometimes peeked at mom and saw that same calm smile on her face. The first night at home, mom and dad said night-night and walked me to my crate. I went right in. I didn't cry or whine or fuss ANY………I just walked in, laid down, and went to sleep. I slept all night. In the morning, dad got me up and took me outside to MY SPOT. I peed and pooed real quick. Then I got to eat.

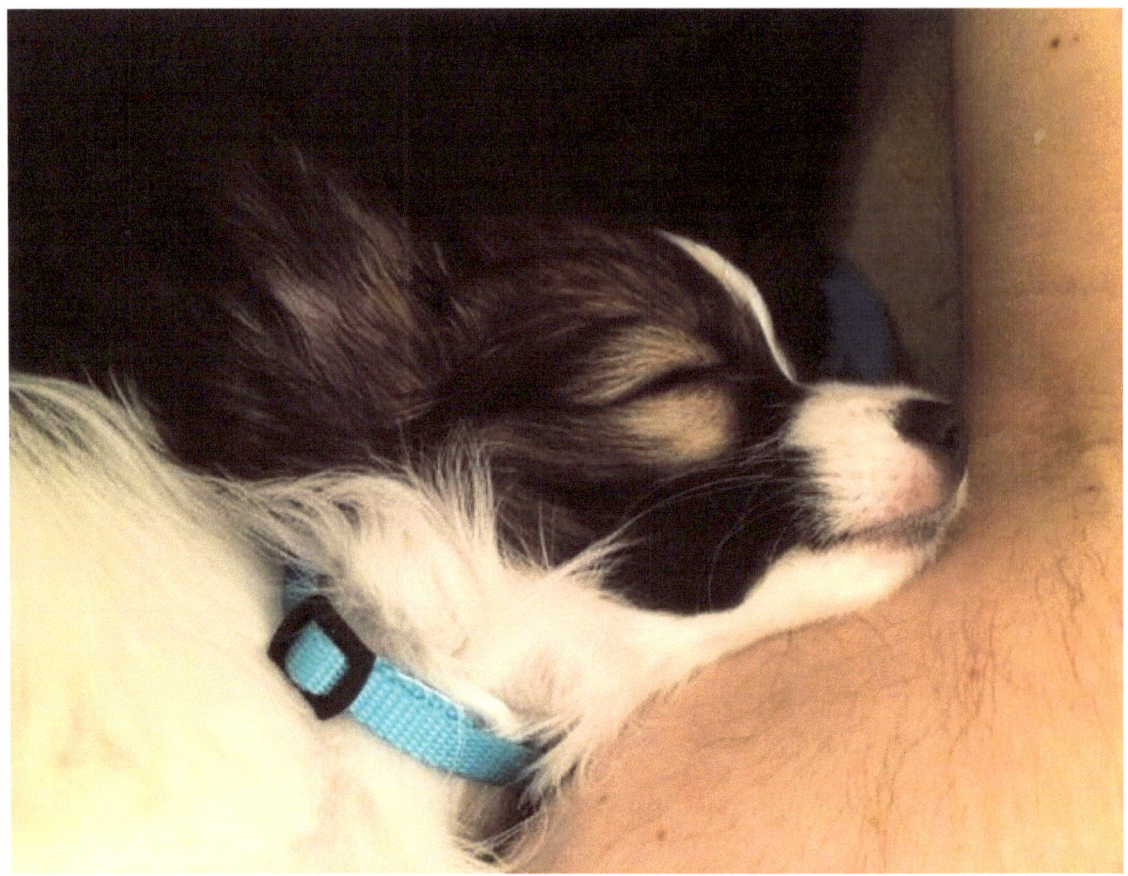

Dad and I always had calm smiles on our faces
when I would sleep resting my head in the crook of his arm

TOE BITING

Soon I taught dad another one of my favorite games—toe biting. I LOVED this game……I'm not sure dad liked it as much as I did though. Very soon after mom and dad got me from Raleigh, dad started to write a book. On the website for his book he has MY picture and he even wrote a dedication to me and called me TOE BITER EXTRAORDINAIRE. Thanks

Hi. I'm Oliver

Dad. I KNEW you really liked my game and were just pretending not to like it. Here's the photo of me that brings to mind my primary toe biting days while dad was writing.

My toe biting photo is also at dad's website:
149 Ways to Wipe Your (sorry, I can't say that word here)

Toe Biter Extraordinaire

SCHOOL

Days passed quickly and it seemed like with each passing day I grew bigger. Very soon I weighed three pounds, then four and then five. Dad could pretty easily pick me up with one hand at the beginning, but I started to get longer so he began picking me up with both hands. We spent our days playing tug, or me playing with one of my squeaky toys, or running in the backyard, or napping. Life was good. My mom and dad loved me very much. Now mom thought that by the time I was three months old it was time to go to school. They thought about naming me Einstein, but they had already named me Oliver. Oliver. This was a pretty serious name so (often) they shortened it to Ollie. Technically, my name is Lacewing Oliver All Over My Heart. Though I didn't become a show dog, my AKC (American Kennel Club) name is Lacewing (my breeder's name) Oliver All Over My Heart. **Lacewing Oliver All Over My Heart.** I LOVE my name!

Now back to school. Say, isn't that the name of a movie with some big guy named Rodney? So mom diligently took me to school every week for months. I went to Puppy 1 and Puppy 2 school and mom studied with me —A LOT. She was very patient and very committed. She taught me (ALMOST) everything I know. I learned how to SIT. I learned how to DOWN. I learned how to STAY. I learned PLACE and WAIT and LET'S GO and COME and LEAVE IT and TAKE IT, and I learned NO. Sometimes I learned a lot of NO, but mostly I learned to be a GOOD BOY, GOOD BOY! I learned how to walk properly, at least when mom was walking with me. Dad is a little more lax, though mom says he is a LOT more lax. I love my MOM and my DAD *very, very* much. Hi MOM! Hi DAD!

PHOTO SHOOTS

Another thing I got to do with my dad was photo-shoots. He bought me special fabrics and would put them on the floor with a toy. I would lie on the fabric and he would take photos of me. Sometimes he would dangle the toy, or hold it in front of me or waive his hand or fingers or call my name and then he would get in funny positions with his camera. I would hear SNAP, SNAP, SNAP, SNAP like a rapid fire gun but a much quieter and friendlier sound. Now, I forgot to tell you something real important, so I better stop and tell you now. I like to keep my tongue out.

MY TONGUE

From the VERY BEGINNING, I liked to keep a little bit of my tongue out. Now not always, but A LOT! My parents wondered if my tongue was too big for me because every now and then, I would keep A LOT of my tongue out. But usually just a little bit showing. I noticed that whenever I did this my parents would do one of two things—they would either smile at me or stick their tongues out back at me. We all liked this. A LOT.

Now, back to the photo-shoot story I was telling you about a minute ago.

All Over My Heart

Dad says that if you look up the definition of cute it says: OLIVER

Dad did photo shoots with red fabric, yellow fabric, green fabric, purple fabric, zebra fabric, leopard fabric and a couple of others. Now you can see from my photos that I have distinctive markings. Some fabrics worked better than others to accentuate my good looks and royal background. Sometimes dad would have a great photo of me, but I was partially off the fabric so the photo wasn't up to snuff. Other times, everything was just right……well *almost* just right……the colors were great, and I was in the right place on the fabric, but the photo was blurry. Oh well. What did we do? We kept trying, that's what we did!

THE PERFECT PHOTO

One of our favorite shoots was with a brown and black animal print fabric because this blended in really well with my markings. Just to be nice to dad, I stuck my tongue out flawlessly. Not too much. Not too little. Just right. This photo was *so* perfect, that dad made HUNDREDS AND HUNDREDS of copies of it and had them printed in 4" X 4" size. He's brought them around the world, locally, and to his work, and has given them to many, many people. He made a website called www.bringingtheworldcloser.com and posted that photo on it. On that website dad wrote: This is Lacewing Oliver All Over My Heart. Isn't he all over yours? As far as "I" can tell the answer is yes because it seems that every person who has ever seen this photo has a giant smile on their face after they get the photo. Well, one guy actually didn't have a smile on his face, but dad said something was mentally wrong with him.

All Over My Heart

People all over the world have gotten this photo, the very same one that dad keeps taped on the walls of his office. He says that he bets everyone who has gotten my photo has it taped somewhere on their wall!! By the way, this photo is the cover of my book, the one you are reading right now.

If you were ice cream dad says I'd make you melt!
….and unless you are that crazy guy, I bet you have a smile on your face right now!!

Aren't *you* glad that I held my tongue out just right for dad, that I was perfectly centered on the leopard print fabric, that I was a good boy and stayed still, and that you too now have my photo here and on the cover of this book? My dad says that if you ever meet him, he has another 4" X 4" photo for you. This is the photo that dad has handed out all over and that really has connected the world. Remember, when you make someone smile, you make a friend.

SPORTS

I also like sports. In particular, I like TENNIS. I like it so much that mom and dad bought me LOTS of tennis balls. I bring the ball to them and they taught me FETCH (which means to drop the ball at their feet or in their hand after I retrieve it). I like to play this game A LOT. When mom and dad bring me to GRAMMY (she's a local breeder and groomer who bred Louie and Miss Molly, mom and dad's first dogs) she doesn't play fetch, so when I get back home I make dad play more often than usual to make up for the fetch I missed and otherwise would have gotten to play.

I actually like baseball too. You see, I am a great CATCHER. When mom or dad throw my tennis ball, I can catch it on a bounce. I can catch it high or catch it low. I can catch it with one bounce or two bounces or even three bounces. I'm also a speed walker. I prance back with the ball almost like I was in a show and if I was, I would *always* be TOP DOG.

Though I really love TENNIS and BASEBALL they can sometimes be frustrating. You see sometimes the ball goes under a piece of furniture or behind it and I can't get to it. It doesn't really matter that I have 5 or 6 *other* balls on the floor readily visible. When I've been biting on one, *that's* the one I want. So when this happens, I cry and you know what happens then? Dad almost always gets it for me. The same thing happens when the ball passes between the metal bars of the gates in our kitchen. Then the ball escapes into the living room and I have to cry and whimper and repeatedly scratch the gate so dad will get the ball we were playing with.

Tennis anyone?
And remember, I like baseball too!

Hi. I'm Oliver

(Hi)

GRAMMY

GRAMMY (Darlene Bosch) and Dawn take care of me sometimes when mom and dad go away or sometimes when GRAMMY misses me, or sometimes (rarely) when mom and dad are home but have something going on that they won't be able to care for me for a day or two. I like GRAMMY. I really like when I get to GRAMMY'S house when I haven't been there in a while. But when mom turns around and walks away I always bark at her saying—Mom? MOM? **MOM!!!!!!!!!!!!** I thought we were just saying *hi* to GRAMMY. You're not *leaving* me with GRAMMY are you?! Where are you going? Mom? MOM? **MOM!!!** It's ok though because there are cats at GRAMMY'S and one of them likes me A LOT. We play together. Sometimes at GRAMMY'S I get my hair done. I get washed and shampooed and dried and coiffed. COIFFURE…. French…. like PAPILLON!! Oui Oui. Oui Oui mon aimee, J'aime m'appelle Ollie.

COOKING

Another pastime is cooking. My dad likes to cook and I like to help. Sometimes I like to help a little too much. So usually dad makes me DOWN and stay 10 or 20 feet away from him. He doesn't want me to get hurt. I REALLY like to watch him cook, ESPECIALLY when he cooks noodles. That's because I like to EAT noodles. Dad has created a game with noodles. The game is, he carefully moistens a long noodle like spaghetti. He does this by putting it in his mouth and moistening it with his tongue. He puts it in his mouth slowly so it doesn't get knotted or anything. Then he leaves just a very small bit hanging out of his mouth and he gets down on his knees and says *nice….nice*, which means I have to sit, not jump, and be calm (I HATE being calm, but if it means getting a noodle, I'm a GOOD BOY!). I gently get up to dad's mouth, the noodle hanging out from it and start to suck it down little by little. Sometimes I even kiss him before I take the noodle. We're about an inch apart from one another, the noodle going into my mouth and out of dad's. Sometimes he cooks a VERY SPECIAL noodle for me. They are called LONGevity noodles and they are made in Thailand. These noodles are special because they are about 5 or 6 feet long. When dad puts one of these in his mouth and I eat it out of his mouth it takes a while just to eat ONE noodle. And I almost never just get to eat *one* noodle. Usually I get two or three and dad saves some for the next couple of days too! How much fun is this!!!!!!

BED!!!!! (and how I miss it)

During most of the two years that I have lived with mom and dad I have slept in my crate. However, on two occasions I have gotten to sleep in bed with them. We used to have date nights…….those were special nights, once or twice a week, when I would get to sleep with mom and dad. Two other times I got to sleep with mom and dad for about a month in a row. A MONTH IN A ROW! Unfortunately I had a couple of accidents in their bed (and peed). They were NOT happy and that ended my extended stay bed sleeping. Sorry mom and dad. **I DIDN'T MEAN IT**. Now when I DID get to sleep with mom and dad I would usually start out the night between mom's legs. She sleeps facing up and I would have a nice blanket to sleep on that was on top of the bed. I would nuzzle between her legs and be a good boy and sleep. Sometime later, usually an hour or two into the night, I would move over to dad's (I mean **MY** side of the bed). I would usually sleep nuzzled behind his legs. Dad sleeps on his side and this creates a perfect space for me. I might be small, but I am strong and I push up right against dad's legs. While dad is asleep, and unaware, I push up against him. First across his legs. Then across his butt. Then across his back. Then across his head and miraculously, I am able to push dad over practically to the side of the bed. Not *off* the bed, but close. This way, I can **really** spread out crossways. It's a good thing that mom and dad have a king-size bed. Seemingly, when I did get to sleep in their bed (not anymore) "I" was the KING of the bed. Dad didn't seem to mind that I didn't let him have much space. He liked me being up against him.

Sometimes at the start of the night, before dad fell asleep, he would be on his back and I would lay up against his side next to his chest and he would hold me next to him. We were sleeping buddies. Later in the night is when I would push him onto his side and then push him over so I had LOTS AND LOTS of room for myself. Again, dad never seemed to mind. I love you MOM. I love you DAD. Thanks for letting me sleep in your bed for the time that you did. Those are some of my favorite memories growing up—except for the two times I had an accident. I **REALLY** am sorry. It's ok though, because I like my crate a lot. I REALLY like that mom and dad make my blankets all nice and fluffy just right before I get in my crate so I can crumple them up and move them just the way I like them. Mom is VERY generous. She's bought me stacks of blankets. Sometimes, if one gets dirty, they wash it and fluff it up again. And sometimes, they throw it away and I get a new fresh fluffy beautiful blanket! I love blankets, new ones, old ones, fresh ones, used ones, clean ones, and dirty ones.

WORK

Dad gets up at 5:20AM to go to work and he says, "I gotta get up Ollie," so I can make some money to buy you new blankets. And food. And treats. And cookies. And bones. And toys. And crates. And bed covers. And poo poo bags. And medicines. And insurance. My dad says that he would get up at **4:20AM** if he had to so that he could provide for mom and me. Fortunately, he doesn't have to do that.

GARDENING

Recently, my dad started a garden for the first time in years. He loved to have a vegetable garden at the house he and mom used to live in, but unfortunately our current house has trees and grass in most of the sunny areas. In fact the only real area that doesn't have trees and grass and gets enough sun is our back, two-tiered deck, so this year he started his garden there. It's a container garden. He worked hard to get our planters all beautiful. He took out the old soil and put nice fresh miracle grow moisture control soil in the planters and in containers. You should have seen dad the time he was changing out some soil and came across a baby black snake in the soil. That time I must say he moved even faster than I do when I'm playing NASCAR. Now dad is pretty strong and he could probably do the gardening on his own, but he is much better with me. I watch him through our screened porch and make sure he is doing it right. So far, he's been pretty much right on. Sometimes when I watch dad I get distracted…

DISTRACTIONS AND BARKING

I may be small, but I have a VERY BIG brain. It's always doing something (unless I am sleeping). Sometimes it is following commands that I learned—like SIT, DOWN, STAY, COME. The top things that distract me are door bells, people, and animals, especially squirrels. Sometimes I think that the squirrels are taunting me. They stare at me so much that I want to chase them. I try to do this, but I'm always on a leash and dad won't let me chase them. If I could just get off the leash……I would show those squirrels who is boss. SILLY SQUIRRELS! I also get distracted with anyone (besides my mom and dad) who walks out the back of our house, especially if they are walking down a pier or out by their boat. Then I give them a good bark. I used to watch the birds feeding at the bird feeder right outside our breakfast area of the kitchen. Ultimately, mom and dad had to move the bird feeder farther away from the house or I would bark too much.

Now speaking of BARKING, I never barked, not even once when my parents picked me up or drove me home or got me home. In fact, I never barked for weeks and weeks. It was so unusual that my mom and dad wondered if I COULD bark. When the first bark came, it was quite a surprise, because I had a bigger bark than the size of my small body. I showed mom and dad that I was a BIG BOY!!!!! Mostly, I just bark as a guard dog, especially when I see things out the back window of our home, but also at the front door, *especially* at the UPS man (dad calls the guy the Amazon Prime Man), or when I see other dogs. Otherwise, I'm pretty quiet. Well, pretty quiet, meaning I don't bark. But I do have many other voices in addition to my bark.

VOICES

One voice is the one I have when I'm told to do something that I *don't* want to do. Like when I bark at a squirrel outside the window, or at a bird, and mom or dad say: "NO." Then they say: "NIGHT-NIGHT," meaning I have to go to my crate (door open though). As I do, I give them a little chirp. This is my way of saying……REALLY? Do I have to REALLY go to my crate? FINE. Then when they say: "DOWN," I chortle a few more chirps back at them until they say: "DOWN," again. Then I comply. I do my same type of chortling and chirping when mom or dad aren't paying (enough) attention to me and I want to play. Like sometimes they are reading or watching TV and I bring one of my favorite tennis balls up to them, so we can play fetch. I nudge them a little, and they almost always start playing with me—especially dad…….he is a pushover most of the time…….LOVE YA DAD!

ACTIVITIES, MALE BONDING, & MOVIES

Me and dad have a few other things we do regularly. Of course he takes me out when I need to go (you know, to relieve myself). Unlike most dogs, I don't pee IN the grass. I have to first check about 30 or 40 spots before I decide which one is the best to pee in. Though I often walk *within* the grass, I *almost* never pee in the middle of the grass. I like to find the perfect spot at the *edge* of the grass where the grass meets a sidewalk or edge of a driveway. This way the pee can run down it instead of just onto the grass.

I've also shown dad a special form of exercise that I invented. I'm aware that humans play spin the bottle. I have a little version of this myself. I call it spin the butt or pivot and poo. When I poo, I like to pivot a few times. Dad doesn't know this, but it requires a special core exercise and coordination to do this. He thinks I just do it for fun, but actually it is to strengthen my obliques and keep my six-pack abs. Additionally, I'm doing it to help dad. By dropping poops in a variety of places he has to do his own special core exercises just to pick them up.

Another thing that me and dad regularly do together is something that helps us to male bond. This is perhaps my favorite thing to do. Well, almost favorite. Those LONGevity noodles are hard to beat and sleeping in bed was also pretty special, but this thing we do to male bond is pretty darn fun. Dad sits on the floor in a special spot so that his legs are out straight

Elk antlers—are these cool or what!

and his back is up against the wall. The special spot for this is a few feet over from my dog bowls. When he does this it's basically a signal that we are going to male bond. I scurry around the kitchen, look at a tennis ball, sometimes pick it up, and then drop it. I scurry a little more and find my elk antler, then I bring it over to dad and I lie across his lap. He then *holds* my antler for me and I chew on it. The two of us just get to be with one another, everything else in the world is seemingly shut out. Dad holds me next to him on his lap and pets me with one hand and holds my antler in the other and I go to town on that antler. We often do this before I go to bed, but I tell you, I could do it all day long. I'll even eat the antler out of his hand with him carrying me and walking around. I'm a GOOD BOY!

Say, have you seen any good movies lately? The reason I ask is that I LOVE to watch movies. Me and dad watch them regularly. In fact, whenever dad says, "Ollie, you want to watch a movie?" I run up to the couch and put my front paws on it. By that time, dad has already loaded a movie into our DVD player and put a nice, really soft and really fluffy blanket on the couch next to him. That's *my* movie watching spot. Dad lifts me up and puts me on my bankie and I lie down next to him. I've seen A LOT of movies with dad. If they are scary movies, he holds me so I don't get scared. Now, when I said I've seen A LOT of movies with dad, that's not quite fully true. I've actually seen A LOT of the *starts* of movies. Being on that soft and cushy blanket makes me tired, so usually after a half hour or so, I tend to fall asleep.

When the movie is over, dad shuts off the TV and puts his head down next to me. He very gently pets me and I usually open my eyes (even though I can barely keep them open). We stare at each other and dad lies right next to my side. Me on my side and him on his and we lie facing each other. We do this for a few minutes. I love looking in my dad's eyes as much as he likes looking into mine. Then he asks me if I'm ready to go night-night and he very gently carries me to the bedroom and I go to my crate and almost instantly fall asleep.

GRRR!

The next day, if it's a work day, dad takes me out to pee and poo about 640am. When we come back in, he leaves me in the kitchen and gets his toothbrush so he can brush before heading off to work. While I'm in the kitchen, I find my dog bed near the window, and lie down, because you know what? 640am is *freaking* early and I like to sleep until 9am whenever dad is not working. When he finishes brushing, he says its time for me to go back to my night-night in the bedroom. Now, while he was brushing, I've gotten real comfortable in my dog bed on the floor and I'm not particularly keen on getting out of it. So even if dad is *real* gentle, I give him a growl as he starts to pick me up. If he isn't gentle, I give him a serious GRRRRRRR…..which means leave me alone, I like this soft bed *right* here. OK. FINE. You can bring me back into the bedroom! As soon as dad has picked me up and has me in his arms, I let out a big yawn and dad continues to carry me to my crate in the bedroom. He kisses mom goodbye and says see you later Ollie. I can't wait until he comes home.

I've got an internal clock and know the usual time he gets back home. If he is late ANY, I just stay at the back gate and stare at the door to the garage. DAD? DAD? DAD? Where are you? FINALLY, he's home and I am SO happy. Hi DAD! Hi DAD! Hi DAD! I am so happy to see you. I jump and bark and sometimes go into figure eights. Then, I know it's time for dinner. And we have a special routine here too.

MANNERS & PRAYER

Mom and Dad have raised me with good manners. ESPECIALLY mom. She sets the tone, tells dad this is the way we are going to do it, and he tries to follow her lead. For instance, we pray before meals. Mom and Dad pray before their meals and they pray with me before mine. When they get my food in my bowl and walk over to my dog bowl holder they stare at me and I know it's time to pray. So I go into DOWN position all on my own. Mom taught me this, and ever since she did, I do it. She can convey down for our prayer just by looking at me. Dad can too. I usually can pay attention when they say: "Dear Heavenly Father," but a little after that I get distracted. As soon as they say, "In Jesus' name we pray" and JUST BEFORE they say, "AMEN," I stand up and know it's time to eat. We always say thanks for the food I have and for mom and dad and for the blessings the three of us have which are too numerous to count. They always give thanks for me being in their life and I give thanks for them in mine. And we pray that we are all a blessing to others. I WUF them very, very much. Say, it's getting late isn't it? Why it's almost my bed time.

It's already 9pm. I'm tired. I usually want to go to my night-night about this time so I better end here. And maybe this is the place to end my story for now. Perhaps it is no accident that the last thing I got to tell you about is how we pray before I eat and give thanks for what each of us has. I'm VERY glad my Mom (Hi MOM!) taught me this. It reminds me, and it should also remind YOU, of everything that *you* should be thankful for. NIGHT-NIGHT and thanks for listening to my story. Oh, and thanks to dad for typing for me.

Oliver All Over My Heart. Aren't I all over YOURS?

Part II

A few dog pictures and stories

Hi. I'm a sled dog. I run the Iditarod races in Alaska. Ollie's mom and dad saw me near Juneau, Alaska and I helped to pull their sled, along with some of my buddies. To get to see me and my pals you have to take a helicopter excursion and it can be a little expensive (ok, fine, a lot of expensive). Remember my picture and then remember this lesson:

Never miss a once in a lifetime opportunity.

My owner likes taking me for rides (San Francisco). Remember this:

Take time to smell the roses (and pee on the fire hydrants).

Hi. We are a few dogs just going out for a walk with our dog walkers in San Francisco. Are we well behaved or what! Here's our lesson for you:

BIG DOG or LITTLE DOG, everybody is special.

Hi. We are two dogs that just met. We want to remind you to:

Choose your friends wisely.

Out for a stroll in San Francisco.

We'd both like to remind you:

Be nice to others

and they will want to be your friend.

We saw Oliver's mom while she was pregnant with Oliver at a dog show in Concord, North Carolina in 2015. Walking down one of the aisles, Ollie's dad saw us and we were adoggable, so he took our picture. Remember:

Hang with the right crowd.

Bring on the dog show! And remember:

If you've got it, flaunt it!

This is Hanoi, Vietnam and my photo demonstrates a simple concept.

People everywhere are the same.

The bark of a dog is the same in *all* languages.

Likewise, *people* are also the same everywhere.

Only the superficial, external things are different.

What *matters* is the same.

Unconditional love is what I give. I am Oliver and I am a reminder that:

God spelled backwards is dog. Like God, dogs give <u>unconditional</u> love.

I thought you'd like to see just a few more pictures of me before you finished reading…..

Dad bought me this new blanket since I did such a good job writing this book!

Dad made me stay up late many nights editing the book…..I'm tired dad, can we finish tomorrow?

Love and kindness and everything that is good….

Playing NASCAR with my dad (Hi DAD!)

Running with the wind……

Elk antlers, blankies, toys, playing NASCAR, male bonding, eating noodles…..some people might think that I was spoiled……what do you think?

…Look out for me on the Ellen DeGeneres show.

P.S. that's me below with my bags packed and ready to fly to Burbank, California where you have your show Ellen.

Ellen? Ellen! **ELLEN!**

Have YOUR people call MY people!

Alexa buy another copy of Hi. I'm Oliver!!

About the Author and his Dad

Ollie was born in Raleigh, North Carolina. His MOM (hi MOM!) and DAD (hi DAD!) picked him up when he was two months old and are raising him in the Lake Norman area of North Carolina. When he is not writing, Ollie is probably playing tennis or chewing on his elk antler, or napping, or running figure eights or barking at the UPS man.

While not typing for Ollie, his dad is a dermatologist and lives with his wife Sheri, who is the ringleader of their trio. She sets the rules for Ollie and Dad, and they both try to follow them.

P.S. Since I did such a good job on my book, guess what? Mom (Hi MOM!) and Dad (Hi DAD!) have let me have date nights again in their bed. HOW COOL IS THIS!!

WUF WUF WUF

www.ingramcontent.com/pod-product-compliance
Lightning Source LLC
Chambersburg PA
CBHW060756090426
42736CB00002B/53